Other titles by **SHARNY & JULIUS**

Never Diet Again: Escape the diet trap forever

Fit, Healthy, Happy Mum: How my quest for perfect breastmilk helped me lose 24 kilos in only 8 weeks after the birth of my fourth child

FITlosophy 1: Chasing physical perfection in the world of gluttony

FITlosophy 2: Embracing excellence in the world of mediocrity

Healthy JUNK: Healthy versions of your favorite junk foods

Healthy JUNK 2: 50 more guilt-free delicious recipes

Fit, Healthy, Happy Kids: A food and exercise blueprint for children under 12

Fertile: Understanding babymaking

PregFit: How I finally had a fit, healthy, happy pregnancy and pain-free birth

The Math Diet: The simple step by step guide to carb cycling

Where Have All The Pixies Gone?

Inspire: Transformations from Sharny and Julius' Program

NOURISH

**RECIPES AND INSPIRATION BY MEN AND WOMEN
WHO HAVE DONE OUR PROGRAMS**

Nourish by SHARNY ⧢ JULIUS

www.sharnyandjulius.com

email: sharnyandjulius@sharnyandjulius.com

Copyright © the Kieser Publishing Trust

First published by Kieser Publishing Trust in February 2019

The moral rights of the authors have been asserted. The stories, suggestions and opinions of the authors are their personal views only, and they are simply that, just stories, not historical accounts. The strategies and steps outlined in the book may not work for everyone. Due diligence and thorough research is always recommended.

Photography: Sharny and Julius

Typesetting and Design: Sharny and Julius

ISBN: 978-0-9876378-0-2

TABLE OF CONTENTS

SHARNY JULIUS

SHARNY & JULIUS

FOREWORD

Nothing, nothing comes close to the power of a community. A group of people dedicated to the same thing.

We are so so proud of everyone in our community and we're excited to celebrate and share some of their recipes so they can inspire and benefit you.

We hope that this book serves as a springboard for your own life success, because fitness and health are a metaphor for your entire life. What you achieve here echoes through the rest of your life. What you struggle with here shows up in other areas.

We truly hope through this book that you can see the opportunity more clearly. You are just like us. All the people you'll see in here started where you are right now.

If we can do it, and they can do it, then you absolutely can. Let this book and these wonderful people remind you every day that if you really want it, you'll make it happen.

Lots of love,
Sharny and Julius

HOW TO USE THIS BOOK

We have assembled the recipes as logically as possible, but even then we thought we could make it even easier.

On each recipe, you will find these icons so you can quickly and easily choose a recipe to copy.

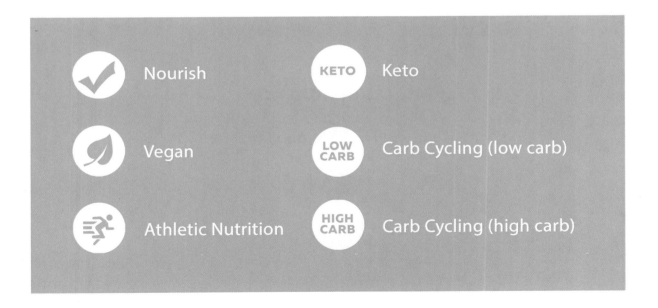

✔	Nourish	KETO	Keto
🍃	Vegan	LOW CARB	Carb Cycling (low carb)
🏃	Athletic Nutrition	HIGH CARB	Carb Cycling (high carb)

My easy go to breakfast or lunch if fasting longer, for carb cycling.

INGREDIENTS:
- 1 egg
- Coconut oil
- Chicken breast baked
- 1/4 small avocado diced
- Red pepper sliced
- Cherry Tomatoes sliced
- Baked activated almonds (seed allowance)
- Raw red onion sliced
- Lettuce

VINAIGRETTE:
- 1 tsp apple cider vinegar
- 1 tsp dijon mustard
- Splash of lemon juice
- 1/4 tsp sea salt

METHOD:
Bake chicken breast. Fry 1 egg over easy in a smudge of odourless coconut oil. Assemble salad and top with shredded or sliced chicken breast. Mix vinaigrette ingredients together and drizzle over the top. Enjoy!

"I feel so healthy and I now have energy because of this journey. It has taught me that consistency and eating right is the way to achieve your goals as well as doing the workouts!"

Maria Kovats

I have lost all track of time on this amazing, life changing journey which has become a permanent daily way of life. I have already reached goal at the end of round 1. I have now lost a total of 11 kilos and current and final weight is 54 kgs for 5'4 ft. Starting weight was 65 kg. I feel so healthy and I now have energy because of this journey. It has taught me that consistency and eating right is the way to achieve your goals as well as doing the workouts!

I no longer care about the scale anymore, this journey is everything. It has opened up my mind, my soul, I have self-love and self-care, I can now even take photos without makeup which I was always hiding behind. I may be turning 50 in November but it is really only a number. I finally feel like I have shed all the negativity and self loathing and that is a beautiful thing. Never be afraid of bettering yourself, on the inside and out!

TRISH'S ZUCCHINI AND BACON SOUP

INGREDIENTS:
- 4 zucchinis
- 4 pieces additive free bacon
- 2 celery stalks
- 5 cups of water

METHOD:
Chop all up, bring to the boil, then simmer for 30mins. Blitz and serve! How easy is that?

HANNAH'S ASIAN TUNA SALAD

INGREDIENTS:
- Tuna
- Button mushrooms
- Asparagus sautéed in a pan with some crushed garlic
- Chilli
- Coriander
- Coconut aminos
- Lemon juice

METHOD:
Serve on a salad bed of spinach, fresh coriander, spring onion, cucumber, 1/4 tomato, and a small tin can of tuna in spring water. Yum!

INGREDIENTS:

- 2x handfuls of mixed leafy greens (unlimited)
- Grated zucchini
- 4x small cherry tomatoes
- 1m / 2 tbsp pepitas
- 1tsp linseed
- Fresh herbs of choice
- Nutritional yeast
- Tahini (seed allowance)

INGREDIENTS FOR DRESSING:

- 4 tbsp ACV (organic)
- A squeeze of lemon juice / 2 tbsp
- Crushed garlic (optional)

METHOD:

Mix tahini, lemon juice (crushed garlic) to make dressing. Assemble salad and top with shre ded chicken. Drizzle with dressing, fresh herbs, and nutritional yeast.

VIVIE'S CHILLI TUNA WITH GREENS

INGREDIENTS:
- Raw broccoli
- Snow peas
- Kale
- Cucumber
- Spring onion
- Tuna
- Organic tomato paste
- Red chilli powder
- Apple cider vinegar

METHOD:
Marinate tuna overnight with organic tomato paste and red chilli powder. Mix with the greens with apple cider vinegar as dressing.

CAROLINE'S BABA GANOUSH

INGREDIENTS:
- Aubergine / eggplant
- Garlic
- Lemon juice
- Salt and pepper
- Parsley
- Tahini

METHOD:
Roast whole aubergine until really soft, blend with garlic, lemon juice, salt, pepper, parsley, and tahini. The amounts depend on you and your preference.

INGREDIENTS (BONE BROTH):

- Wombok
- Bok Choy
- Cabbage
- Parsley
- Spinach
- 2 x Eggs
- Sauerkraut

METHOD:

Make your own both broth as per your recipe.

Boil 2 litres of water with 2-4 tablespoons of brothconcentrate (depending how you like it.)

Add greens wombok, bok choy, cabbage, parsley, spinach and boil until veggies are soft.

Crack 2x eggs straight into boiling water to poach.

Serve topped with Sauerkraut.

Season to taste.

NICOLE'S ZESTY SALMON AND VEGGIE CRUNCH

INGREDIENTS:
- Salmon
- Broccoli
- Snow peas
- Red cabbage
- Coriander
- Spring onion
- Red Capsicum
- Carrot
- Baby spinach
- Small drizzle of lemon

METHOD:
Chop veggies and put into a food processor. Top it off with some cooked salmon. Sprinkle with salt and pepper to taste.

RECIPE INSPIRATION:
Get your tomato fix along with broccoli, celery, red pepper, wilted spinach, perfectly hard boiled eggs and butter crunch lettuce, complete with green onion. Top with a tahini/lemon juice/salt combo! Highly recommend as a lover of food.

CLAUDIA'S BROCCOLI SOUP WITH SPICED CHICKEN BREAST

INGREDIENTS:
- Broccoli
- Chicken breast
- Smoked capsicum, salt, and pepper for flavor

METHOD:
Cook broccoli in water with a dash of salt then purée and add pepper. Spice the chicken breast with smoked capsicum, salt, and pepper. Top with chicken and serve!

SARAH'S VEGAN NOURISH "TACO" SALAD

INGREDIENTS:
- Romaine lettuce
- Grilled peppers
- Garlic
- Cumin
- Black beans
- Fresh homemade guac!
- Add homemade (or fresh sugar free) salsa if
  eating before 2:00 pm

METHOD:
Combine all ingredients. Enjoy!

INGREDIENTS:

- 1 tsp coconut oil
- 2 cloves of garlic, diced
- 1 yellow onion, chopped (don't use for Nourish)
- 2 carrots, diced (substitute zucchini for Nourish)
- 1 can diced tomatoes (fire roasted are really good)
- 4 Cups fresh spinach
- 1/4 Cup dried lentils
- 1 can black beans, drained and rinsed
- 1 tsp chili powder
- 1 tsp cumin
- ½ tsp black pepper
- ½ tsp sea salt
- ½ tsp crushed red pepper flakes
- 4 Cups vegetable broth
- Cilantro and avocado (for garnish)

METHOD:

Sautée garlic in coconut oil (and onion and carrots, if using). Add remaining ingredients, stir and cover.

Bring to boil, reduce heat to a simmer and cook until lentils are tender, approximately 25-30 minutes.

Top with cilantro and diced avocado (optional).

CHARLOTTE'S CHICKEN SOUP

INGREDIENTS FOR STOCK:
- Chicken frame
- Water
- Salt and peppercorn
- Large chunks of celery
- Carrots and leek
- 2 bay leaves

METHOD:
Boil this, simmer, then drain, keep the stock in a seperate pot (you can keep or throw the leftover vegetables).

To make the soup filling, lightly fry some shallots and garlic in a teaspoon of coconut oil. Add diced garlic, shallots, celery, leek, broccoli, caulflower, courgette, brussel sprouts, (greens of choice) and carrot (optional). Season to taste and add the stock back in and add in chicken breast.

ALYSSA'S NOURISH SHRIMP STIR FRY

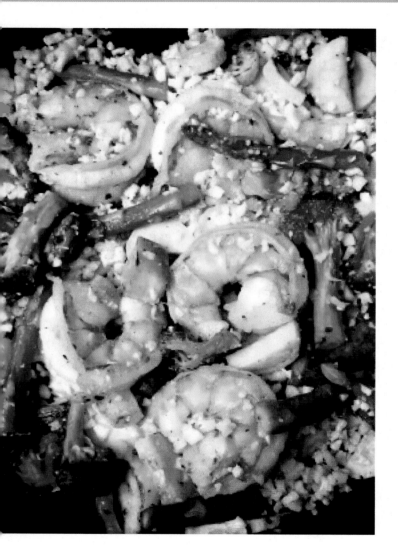

INGREDIENTS:
- Shrimp
- Squash
- Broccoli
- Asparagus
- Garlic
- Basil

METHOD:
Sauté shrimp and veggies in 1 tsp coconut oil.

Roast raw cauliflower rice on a baking sheet until it starts to brown.

Put cauliflower rice in a bowl and pour all the veggies and shrimp over the cauliflower rice.

Yummy!

SHARNY ❤ JULIUS

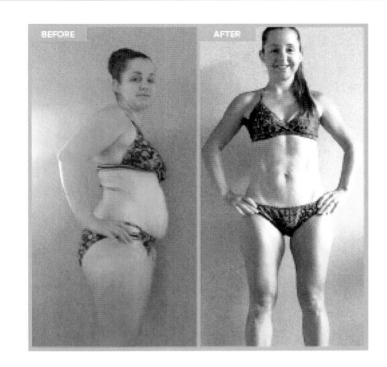

"I am so in love with the way I feel when I exercise my body and feed it good healthy nutritional food!"

Alyssa Keyes

It has been 10 months since I jumped on this fitness train!! I have not looked back since, it actually set me on a fitness and wellness path! And not only have been I been able to maintain my weight but I have used the programs dietary plan and workout style to tone up since my 16 weeks ended! I am so in love with the way I feel when I exercise my body and feed it good healthy nutritional food! My IBS is cured and my gut health is better than ever. My hormonal acne is gone and my skin glows. Not only that but I feel confident and actually can say that I love my body! I am now learning to listen to my body a feed it the food it is designed to process!

So if you are on the fence about this program, just take it from me!!! A FIT LIFE IS A HAPPY LIFE and YOU deserve to be happy and Healthy!! I haven't felt or looked this good since I was 17!!! This was my 30th birthday present to myself!! The best thing I have ever given myself was the gift of a Happy, Healthy, Fit Life!!

LOW CARB

INGREDIENTS:

- Chicken breast
- Grated onions
- Grated carrots
- Grated spinach
- Grated cauliflower

METHOD:
Blend them together, then shape into balls. Dry pan fry, the enjoy!

This is my fave recipe for breakfast or lunch!

INGREDIENTS:

- 1 x tsp coconut oil
- Cauliflower (riced)
- Zucchini diced
- Red Capsicum diced
- Yellow Capsicum diced
- Rhindless bacon diced
- Eggs
- Garlic
- Salt
- Additive free organic smoked paprika

METHOD:

Add coconut oil to hot pan .
Fry all ingredients.
Enjoy! Super simple!

JILL'S TURKEY BURGER TORTILLAS

INGREDIENTS:

- Cauliflower Tortillas (make your own)
- Ground turkey (grind your own to make sure no additives)
- Homemade taco seasoning (organic and additive free)
- Jalapeños
- Nutritional yeast

METHOD:

Rice cauliflower in food processor I made 4 tortillas. Use your own recipe for tortilla.

Grind Turkey burger with homemade organic taco seasoning.

Pan fry turkey mixture on the grill with jalapeños and nutritional yeast for cheese.

Top tortillas with turkey mix and leafy greens of choice. Amazingly good!!!

STEPH'S BACON AND LEEK BAKED CAPSICUM

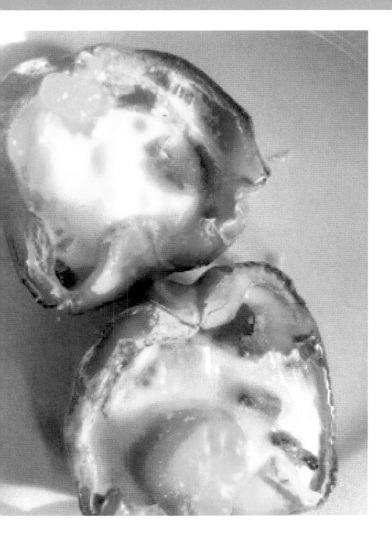

INGREDIENTS:

- Capsicum
- Shortcut bacon (additive free, good quality, and rhindless)
- Leeks
- Coconut oil

METHOD:

Preheat oven 200c.

Half capsicum and put coconut oil on the bottom so it doesnt stick.

Fry the bacon and leek .

Stuff capsicum with fried ingredients.

Top with egg.

Bake for 15 minutes or until the egg is cooked!

HANNAH'S STUFFED SPAGHETTI SQUASH

INGREDIENTS:
- 1/2 small spaghetti squash
- 1x small tin tuna
- Mushrooms (finely chopped)
- Spinach
- Herbs of choice (make sure organic additive free)
- Capsicum
- Asparagus
- Freshly squeezed lemon juice
- Salt
- Pepper

METHOD:
Preheat oven 180 degrees. Halve a small spaghetti squash, place cut side down on tray and bake for approx. 30 mins until softened. For filling, mix together small tin tuna, finely chopped mushrooms, spinach, herbs of choice capsicum and asparagus lemon juice, salt and pepper. Loosen up the "spaghetti" then fill each half with the filling mix, pop back in oven for about 10 mins to heat throughout. Yum!

I'm addicted! The hummus is super easy!

INGREDIENTS:

- 500g zucchini
- Garlic (I use 2 cloves)
- 1/3 cup lemon juice
- 1/3 cup tahini
- Salt and pepper
- Salmon

METHOD:

Roast zucchini, leave them to cool.
Throw all other ingredients in a food processor.
Add cooled zucchini and put into a food processor until you get the consistency you like.
Roll like up in zucchini strips with salmon.
Enjoy!

HANNAH'S EGG WHITE OMELETTE AND GREEN SMOOTHIE

INGREDIENTS (OMELETTE):
- 1/4 cup egg whites
- 100g mushrooms
- 1 cup spinach

METHOD:
Sauté mushroom and spinach with some garlic. Add in egg whites and cover with lid until egg cooked through. While this cooks make the smoothie.

INGREDIENTS (SMOOTHIE):
- 1 cup spinach
- 1 lebanese cucumber
- 1/2 serve approved protein powder
- 5 mint leaves
- 1 tray ice cubes

METHOD:
Blend until smooth

SHARNY ❖ JULIUS

INGREDIENTS:
- Tuna
- Zucchini zoodles
- Red pepper
- Broccoli
- Asparagus
- Spring onion
- Nourish approved basil pesto

METHOD:
Roast red pepper, broccoli, and asparagus. Use a spiralizer to make zucchini zoodles. Combine ingredients and top with basil pesto and spring onion.

"I cannot wait to continue to nourish my body with healthy & tasty foods but also continue to build on my strength."

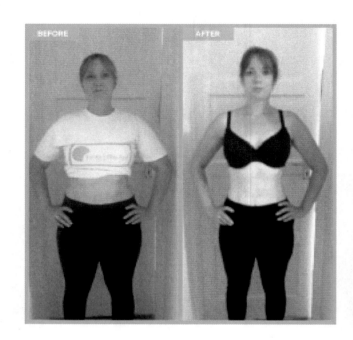

Karoline Gray-Clark

Wow what an amazing journey I've been on thanks to you guys! From being frumpy, grumpy, overtired to becoming a happy & healthier person in just a few weeks!! I relied on coffee, chocolate & all bad foods to get me through the day. I'm only 35 but some days I felt much older as I ached all over. I honestly thought it was just how it was gonna be.

12 weeks ago I signed up after seeing a Facebook ad because I was fed up of buying bigger & bigger clothes. I thought 'f*ck it... Let's try that!' I had no idea that not only would I drop to a weight I haven't seen in years but that I'd actually enjoy it!!! After 8 weeks I'd dropped 12kg!!!! Now I've dropped 2 more & hit my goal.

Thank you to Sharny & Julius for creating an easy to follow programme that has built a healthy lifestyle! I cannot wait to continue to nourish my body with healthy & tasty foods but also continue to build on my strength.

KAROLINE 'S STUFFED BELL PEPPER

I mostly stick with plain chicken & veggies but when I mixed things up I loved...

INGREDIENTS:
- 1 x Bell pepper
- Coconut oil
- Cauliflower rice
- Additive free, good quality shortcut bacon
- Approved veggies of choice (I like mushrooms, courgette & spinach)

METHOD:
Cut top of & remove bell pepper seeds.
Use coconut oil to cook up some veggies of choice with some fat free bacon.
Steam cauliflower rice.
Mix all veggies together & season with pepper or Himalayan salt to taste.
Stuff into pepper & top with slice of bacon.
Grill for 5 mins.
Enjoy!

ALYSSA'S NOURISH SUSHI

INGREDIENTS:
- Cauliflower
- Shrimp
- Avocado
- Cucumber
- Tuna
- Nori sheets

METHOD:
Rice cauliflower by putting cauliflower in the food processor and pulse until you like the consistency. Boil for 3 mins and strain well!

Place on one half of your Nori Paper and fill with whatever you like I put (shrimp, avocado, and cucumber) and it was yummy ! I put some Ahi Tuna in a few but liked the shrimp best. Just cut them into length and place them along one side and roll toward the empty side then wet the edge with water and seal. Then cut them into pieces! Enjoy!

ALYSSA'S SALMON NORI WRAPS

INGREDIENTS:
- 2 organic nori papers
- 3 tbs of cooked riced cauliflower
- Chopped spinach
- A few bunches of micro greens
- One half sliced cucumber
- Few pieces of wild Alaskan sliced smoked salmon (with no added sugar or salt)
- 1 tsp of tahini
- Grated ginger
- A little sprinkle of coconut aminos

METHOD:
Fold in to a wrap with a simple salad on the side of microgreens, cilantro, 3 small tomatoes.
Add a sprinkle of ACV with pinch of little pink Himalayan sea salt.

Serve with a big glass of H2O with a squeeze of lemon! Hope you like it because it was AMAZING!! Best lunch I have made in a while!

NICK'S FAVE BREAKFAST FRY UP

INGREDIENTS:

- Coconut oil
- 2x eggs
- Peppers
- Mushrooms
- Spring onions
- 2 x cherry tomatoes
- Massive handful of spinach
- Nutritional yeast
- Himalayan salt and pepper to taste
- Turkey bacon (additive free)

METHOD:

Fry the eggs (in a little coconut oil with a saucepan lid on so it's not soggy) with peppers, mushrooms, spring onions, cherry tomatoes & spinach. Sprinkle with pink Himalayan salt, black pepper. Cover it in yeast flakes.

Yum! It's even nicer with a couple of rashers of Turkey bacon!

SHARNY ⊗ JULIUS

INGREDIENTS:

- Asparagus
- Broccoli
- Mushrooms in garlic
- Lemon zest and juice
- Salmon
- Cauliflower
- Homemade almond milk
- Smoked paprika (additive free)

METHOD:

Put everything together in the same pan, cover with lid to help it all cook without burning. Mash 1 cup of cauliflower rice with smoked paprika, a dash of almond milk (in seed allowance amount) and some pink salt. Amazing!

INGREDIENTS:

- Broccoli
- Mushrooms
- Lettuce for shells,
- 1 tomato as salsa
- Baked chicken
- Paprika (additive free organic)
- Garlic powder (additive free organic)

METHOD:

Preheat oven 180 degrees.
Coat chicken & veggies in spice (except tomato).
Bake in oven with a little coconut oil.
Once cooked, shred the chicken.
Top lettuce with baked veggies, chicken and tomato.

Enjoy!

It makes quite a bit more than you see in the photo. It's basically Sharny's smoothie recipe but juiced.

INGREDIENTS:

- 1 cucumber
- 2 zucchini (I often use just one, otherwise it's just too much to drink)
- 4 broccoli florets
- 6 kale leaves
- 3 celery stalks
- And juice from 1/4 lemon

Tips:

I sometimes add a few romaine lettuce leaves as it's really good for you and like the flavor. I really like this juice! At first it was a tiny bit tough as it's not sweet but I look forward to it now!

TAN'S BACON, SWEET POTATO, AND ZUCCHINI FRITTERS

INGREDIENTS (MAKES 8):

- 4x rashers shortcut bacon diced (additive free)
- 1/2 large sweet potato grated
- 1x medium zucchini grated
- Handful of greens (spinach & kale)
- 6x eggs (add more if you need, consistency should be wet)
- Fresh herbs of choice (I added sage, basil would be nice)
- 1 x tablespoon Italian herbs additive free
- Salt to taste

METHOD:

1: Fry off bacon in non-stick frypan .
2: Whisk eggs.
3: Combine all ingredients in a bowl.
4: Place Silicon egg rings in pan , pour mixture in. Place lid on pan and cook until fritters start to look solid, check them by running spatula around the edge and if solid remove egg rings and flip to fry other side.
Serve with leafy greens such as spinach & kale!

DEARNE'S THAI TURKEY BALLS & CABBAGE

INGREDIENTS:
- Turkey Mince (make into balls)
- Chilli
- Ginger
- Garlic
- Coriander
- Cabbage
- Coconut aminos

METHOD:
Make turkey mince into balls with chilli, ginger, garlic and coriander.
Steam.
Soak cabbage in Apple cider Vinegar and salt
.
Use coconut aminos as a dipping sauce.
Enjoy!

RECIPE IDEA:
Chicken grilled with chilli and garlic. Chopped green bean, courgette and spinach pan fried with cauli rice!

KIM'S CHILLI PRAWN ZOODLE STIR FRY

INGREDIENTS:
- Zoodles
- Red onion
- Peppers
- Chilli
- Ginger
- 2 tbsp chopped tomato
- King Prawns

METHOD:
Stir fry all ingredients except zoodles.
Cook down and add zoodles at the end.
Enjoy!

CARA'S SUPERFOOD AND NOURISH FRIENDLY PESTO RECIPE

For ultimate deliciousness, I recommend making up a batch the day before you're going to eat it to allow the flavours to develop to perfection.

INGREDIENTS:
- 1 very generous bunch of fresh basil
- 1 cup baby spinach
- 1 cup kale
- Juice of approx. 1 lemon
- 1/4 cup activated pumpkin seeds
- 30 activated almonds
- 2 cloves crushed garlic
- 1/4 cup nutritional yeast
- 1 tablespoon dulse flakes
- Himalayan salt and freshly cracked pepper to taste

METHOD:
Mix all ingredients in a food processor. Mix a serve with zoodles, as a dip for veggie sticks, dollop on your protein, mix with water & use as a salad dressing or veggie drizzle or however you like! Versatile, nutritious & delicious! Just keep in mind the recipe makes 4 serves & each serve uses your day's almond/seed allowance from your morning snack, if you're on nourish.

Recipe by Kara, photo by Jane

CARA'S NORI HAND ROLLS

INGREDIENTS:
- Broccorice or riced broccoli
- Tuna
- Freshly grated ginger
- Coriander
- Mint
- Chilli
- A dash of apple cider vinegar
- Coconut aminos in a bowl (to hold stuff together without rice)
- A sheet of nori

METHOD:
Add mixed greens and cucumber on top, then rolled the nori. Tasted like a dream - an absolute gamechanger!

INGREDIENTS:
- Chicken breast
- Eggs
- Almond meal (seed allowance)
- Nutritional yeast blend
- Spinach

METHOD:
Spice the chicken breast and dip in egg, then in almond meal (just 2 tbs for 4 chicken breasts) and nutritional yeast blend. You can make it on a pan, in a stove or in an oven.

Put roasted spinach leaves on tray (best not to let them overlap), spray lightly with a bit of coconut oil and spices (I use Himalayan salt and an Italian blend) and bake in oven for 8 minutes at about 180c! So crispy and yummy!

"I have also regained my fitness and on top of it all, I am a much happier and confident person than before!"

Steffi Gregersen

Not only did I lose 36kg (3 rounds extreme and 1 carb cycling) and have been maintaining that for 4 months now, I have also regained my fitness and on top of it all, I am a much happier and confident person than before! I am mentally a million times stronger than last year and I am loving every second of my life!

Right from the start I knew that mindset is the most important thing on this journey and that I need to go in it with a no excuse attitude!

A big thank you to this amazing group of people who had my back in the last year and of course a huge thank you to Sharny and Julius for this amazing program!

SARAH-JANE'S VEGGIE OMELETTE TOPPER

INGREDIENTS:

- Eggs
- Mushrooms
- Zucchini
- Kale
- Red capsicum
- Chilli
- Coconut oil

METHOD:

Sautée mushrooms, zucchini, kale, and red capsicum with chili and coconut oil. Slice egg omelette over dish. Top with activated seeds!

APOLLONIA'S CAULI BREAD TOPPERS

INGREDIENTS:
- Cauliflower bread
- Spinach leaves
- Tuna
- Tahini
- Salt and pepper

METHOD:
Put everything over the cauliflower bread, and squeeze half a lemon on top!

SARAH-JANE'S SPICY GREENS

INGREDIENTS:
- Broccoli
- Cauliflower
- Almonds
- Nutritional yeast

METHOD:
Roast veggies and add spices to taste. Sprinkle almonds and nutritionial yeast. Great comfort food!

SHAE'S TUNA STEAK

INGREDIENTS:
- 100g tuna steak
- Coconut aminos
- Ginger
- Garlic

METHOD:
Marinated 100g of tuna in coconut aminos, ginger & garlic. I sautéed some green veg in the same pan after and poured in the excess marinade. Serious winner!

KYLIE'S FISH OR CHICKEN NUGGETS

INGREDIENTS:
- Seed allowance
- 1 tsp curry powder
- 100% fish fillet or chicken breast

METHOD:
Mix seeds with curry powder. Use as coating for the fish or chicken. Put it on baking paper and bake for about 12-15 mins.

KYLIE'S YUMMY SLUGS

INGREDIENTS:
- Eggplant
- Chicken, diced
- Additive free organic spices
- Garlic
- Cumin
- Coriander
- Paprika

METHOD:
Halve eggplant and roast 20 mins.
Scoop out flesh and chop.
Toast cumin, coriander, paprika.
Add eggplant, sliced roast garlic and fine diced chicken.
Scoop back into the eggplant shells and cook again for about 10 mins.

You could also do an Asian version with ginger, garlic, and spring onions.

INGREDIENTS:
- Cauliflower rice
- Coriander
- Chili
- Egg
- Chopped prawn
- Spring onions
- Minced garlic

METHOD:
This is cauliflower rice made into cakes with coriander, chili, egg, chopped prawn, spring onion.

Bake for about 15 mins
Make cauliflower rice the usual way. Squeeze as much water out as possible.
Add coriander, chilli, minced garlic and an egg, and prawns if you like.
On baking paper, form into cakes or tortillas. Bake for about 7 mins, turn them over and bake for another 7.

"The best thing about this 8 weeks is that I have taken control of my own destiny and stopped making excuses about not having time to exercise. So, thanks a lot!"

Kylie Begg

I am 178cm tall and turned 40 this year. I started out at 71.3kg and today the scales say 62.3kg. I am wearing clothes I haven't worn in 5 years and they feel loose.

I am certainly fitter than I have been in many years. My goal is to keep up this level of exercise, to maintain around this weight and to tone up some more.

The best thing about this 8 weeks is that I have taken control of my own destiny and stopped making excuses about not having time to exercise. I am more mindful about what I eat. I love cooking but I cannot imagine baking and cooking like I used to! I have learned a lot more about healthy alternatives and ingredients. So, thanks a lot!

KYLIE'S CHICKEN MEAT BALLS AND VEGGIE FRITTERS WITH CHILLI SAUCE

INGREDIENTS FOR CHICKEN BALLS:

- Minced chicken
- Garlic
- Salt and pepper
- Spring onion
- Parsley
- Additive free herbs

INGREDIENTS FOR VEGGIE FRITTERS:

- Eggs
- Cauliflower
- Broccoli
- Zucchini
- Spring onion
- Almond meal (seed allowance)

INGREDIENTS FOR CHILI SAUCE:

- Capsicum
- Garlic
- 1/4 tomato
- Chilli and spring onion

METHOD:

For chicken balls, put together minced chicken, garlic, salt, peppers, herbs of choice, spring onion, and parsley. Bake for 20 mins.

For the veggie fritters, whisk egg and add veggies and 2 tablespoons of almond meal and 1/2 tsp additive / aluminum free baking soda. I also added parsley and herbs. Then cook in fry pan with a little coconut oil.

For homemade sauce: Sautée capsicum, garlic, 1/4 tomato, chilli, and spring onion.

RECIPE IDEA:
Poached eggs with ham, tomato, mushrooms and asparagus with a piece of bacon (additive free shortcut bacon) and a side of greens.

Hannah Stephens

I never thought I'd find a program that would get me to where I wanted to be - right where I am now! I have battled with my weight and gut health issues my whole life (think a 12 year old weighing 93kg!) I have tried countless diets, both long and short term, plus had every specialist test done that both western and eastern medicine could throw at me, yet it took this program for me to find that just stripping it all back to basics and just concentrating on what fuels your body with pure nutrition is what I needed! Here are my end of 8 weeks (actually did 9.5weeks) results!

STARTING WEIGHT		RESULT AFTER 9.5 WEEKS	
Weight	75.4kg	66.1kg	- down 9.3kg
Waist	87cm	77cm	- down 10cm
Hips	98cm	89cm	- down 11cm
Thigh	61cm	57cm	- down 4cm
Arm	32cm	28cm	- down 4cm
Body fat %	33.2%	26.1%	- down - 7.1%
Muscle %	32.8%	36.2%	- gained 3.4%
Water %	45.9%	50.8%	- gained 4.9%
Bone %	11.3%	12%	- gained .7%

I am in shock and awe especially of the cm's lost! Just one more shout out of thanks to Sharny and Julius - you guys absolutely rock and I can wholeheartedly say I have never completed another program with such amazing support and overall common sense and realness! Love your honesty and love for everyone and I can't thank you enough for getting me here and where this lifestyle is going to take me!

I tell everyone who will listen about what I'm doing and the support and information I have received from Sharny and Julius as well as the wider fitfam - no could ever regret embarking on this journey!

INGREDIENTS:

- 1 400g tin tuna
- 1 head cauliflower riced, steamed and water drained
- 1/4 cup or 2 egg whites
- 2 cups spinach
- Coriander, chilli, ginger etc as flavours to taste

METHOD:

Put all in food processor and blitz to a thick paste. Divide into 8 patties, 2 patties = 1 serve. Fry patties.

Dry roast mushrooms in oven until softened, build your burgers with your choice of salad filling.

INGREDIENTS:

- 50 grams lean beef/chicken mince
- Mixed salad and veggies of choice
- Seasoning (additive free organic spices):
- Chilli powder
- Cumin
- Onion powder
- Garlic powder
- Salt /pepper
- Oregano
- Cayenne pepper
- Lettuce

METHOD:

Fry off hot ingredients in pan.
Fill lettuce boats.
Enjoy!

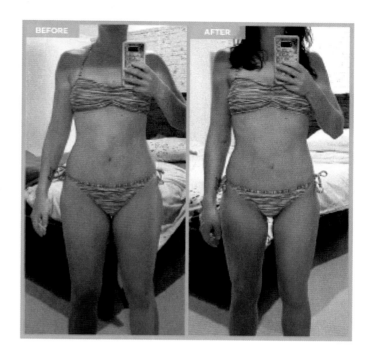

"I am fitter, stronger and more motivated!"

T'leah

I went in to this program thinking that I could lose a little and hopefully feel more confident in myself. I had to give up alot of my favourite things for the 8 week journey that I thought I could NEVER live without (alcohol and chocolate!) to reset my relationship with food. It has been just as much about losing weight and toning as about realising that food is fuel for my body and not for stress, comfort or reward. I am fitter, stronger and more motivated and have spent more time in the kitchen than I have working out, in these last few weeks.

And not a calorie counted AT... ALL.

My total loss is just shy of 8kgs but I have gained so much more than I thought I would on this journey. Thank you Sharny and Julius, even with not a lot to lose, your program works!

KIERA'S SAUTÉED VEGGIES

INGREDIENTS:
- Any greens you have!
- Mushrooms
- Peppers
- 2x Eggs
- Coconut oil

METHOD:
Heat pan with coconut oil.
Sautée green vegetables along with mushrooms and peppers.
Break 2 eggs over the top and scramble them.

INGREDIENTS:
- Eggplant
- Chicken, diced
- Garlic
- Cumin
- Coriander
- Paprika

METHOD:
Cooked chicken warmed up in some coconut oil with pak choi, asparagus, spring onions and chives with a sprinkling of coconut aminos - yum!

RECIPE IDEAS:
This is a great snack idea! Cauli rice made with water, coconut aminos, and lemon juice on a piece of lettuce sprinkled with paprika and cayenne.

INGREDIENTS:
- Cauliflower
- 70g chicken
- Coconut oil
- Seasoning (additive free spices): curry powder, paprika, garlic, and spring onions

METHOD:
Grated cauliflower cooked in coconut oil with curry powder, paprika, some garlic and spring onions. Added the chicken and seasoned to taste. Delicious!

LORIE'S CUCUMBER SLICES

INGREDIENTS:
- Cucumber
- Lemon juice
- Coarse sea salt
- Cayenne pepper

METHOD:

Another great snack idea! Thinly slice some cucumber (I like to peel mine for this). Drizzle slices with a little lemon juice. Sprinkle lightly with coarse sea salt and a little cayenne pepper.

The slight crunch of sea salt, the tart lemon juice and the little bit of heat with the cayenne seems like the perfect combo with the cucumber. YUM!

INGREDIENTS:

- Cauliflower rice
- Lime juice
- Cilantro
- Shrimp
- Seasoning (additive free spices): Cumin, crushed red pepper flakes, garlic

METHOD:

Fry the cauliflower "rice" in a tiny bit of coconut oil, and add a bit of lime juice and cilantro toward the end. Sautée the shrimp in cumin, crushed red pepper flakes, and fresh garlic.

JULIA'S CAULI RICE WITH GARLIC AND DUKKAH

INGREDIENTS:

- 2x soft boiled eggs
- Caulirice
- Garlic
- Dukkah (additive and nut free)

METHOD:

Great snack or quick breakfast idea! Sautée cauli rice with garlic then mix the dukkah. Top with eggs!

LIZZIE'S ZUCCHINI TURKEY BURGER

INGREDIENTS:
- Homemade additive free turkey patties
- Lightly fried zucchini

METHOD:
Just put them together and and season to taste.

"I am loving the exercise, and I have noticed a huge change in my body. This is a way of life for me now, not just an 8 week programme."

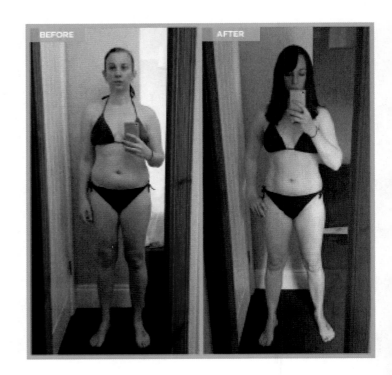

Angie Garnavos

Only 8 short weeks ago, I can still remember how miserable I felt taking those before pictures. The scales told me I was light but my body was weak, I felt tired all time, had no energy, no confidence and no patience. I am so grateful to have seen Sharny's ad about this course, it has changed my life! I have not followed the Nourish Diet completely but I have been eating healthy and my attitude towards food has now completely changed, I no longer crave chocolate or junk food!

I am loving the exercise, and I have noticed a huge change in my body. Thus is a way of life for me now, not just an 8 week programme. Thank you so much Sharny and Julius - you are both truly inspirational!

ANGIE'S LOVELY ROASTED SALMON WITH LEMON & DILL

INGREDIENTS:
- Salmon
- Dill
- Mixed herbs of choice (additive free organic)
- Coconut oil
- Salad greens

Roasted Veggies:
- Sweet potato
- Courgette
- Peppers
- Sprouts
- Mushrooms

METHOD:
Preheat oven to 180 degrees.
Roast salmon in foil with lemon and dill.
Roast veggies and sweet potato with a spray of coconut oil and mixed herbs. Serve with mixed green salad.

Minus sweet potato for Nourish approved!

ANGIE'S CHICKEN STIR FRY

INGREDIENTS:
- Spring onion
- Peppers
- Courgette
- Broccolli
- Chicken
- Mixed spice of choice (additive free organic)

METHOD:
Sprinkle all ingredients with mixed spice and stir fry with a few sprays of coconut oil. Add a little water. Serve on a bed of fresh spinach!

INGREDIENTS:

- Additive free spices
- Basil
- Cumin
- Garlic powder
- Fresh ginger
- Tumeric
- Cardamom
- Curry powder
- Nourish approved veggies of choice

METHOD:

Stir fry in a hot pan and enjoy!

INGREDIENTS:

- Finely grated ginger, garlic, zucchini (squeeze out excess juice), carrot (optional)
- Finely chopped Mushrooms, red capsicum, water chestnuts, kale and coriander.
- Organic chicken mince

METHOD:

Cook in a small amount of coconut oil.

Fry the veggies, ginger, and garlic for a few minutes, then add the chicken and cook through.

Add lots of coriander at the end. Splash in some coconut aminos too! Serve in lettuce leaf with some bean sprouts on top.

INGREDIENTS:

- Portabello mushrooms
- 100% turkey meat, ground
- Chopped spinach/kale
- Chopped zucchini

METHOD:

Stuff the mushrooms withthe turkey and veggies, and flavor with Himalayan salt. Brush them with a little bt of melted coconut oil, then bake! They are delicious!

EMMA'S BABY SALAD

INGREDIENTS:

- A few snow peas
- Cucumber
- Baby spinach
- Snow pea sprouts
- Alfalfa sprouts
- Bean sprouts

METHOD:

Mix together and serve! You can add avocado or lettuce too. I mostly eat this with chicken. Preps easy and stores well!

JESS' DELICIOUS BREAKFAST

INGREDIENTS:
- Zucchini
- Spinach
- Mushrooms
- 2 eggs
- Chilli flakes

METHOD:
Cook veggies together, top with eggs, and serve!

TAN'S NOURISH PATTIES

INGREDIENTS:

- 100g chicken breast (or fish)
- Nourish approved greens of choice
- Fresh Coriander
- Fresh Basil
- Salt
- Pepper
- Tahini
- Organic additive free spices of choice

METHOD:

Whizz all ingredients up in a food processor.
Use hands, make into patties
Fry in a non stick pan.
Serve on top of a bed of salad.
Drizzle with tahini (seed allowance)
Yum!

"I am feeling amazing now compared to where I was, and I have energy and vitality!"

Tania Jago

This program has changed my life entirely.

I embarked on the journey in with a goal of shedding 20kg. I lost 31kg, became a runner AND saved myself. Prior to the program I had anxiety, no energy (and I was starting to have a couple more wines than usual).

I am feeling amazing now compared to where I was, and I have energy and vitality! My health has improved so much. I look forward to a longer and better quality of life!

Thank you to Sharny and Julius and our Fit community, where lives are changed forever!

INGREDIENTS:
- Sliced sweet potato
- Spinach
- Cabbage
- Mushrooms
- Chicken breast strips
- Lettuce

METHOD:
Stir fry spinach, cabbage, mushrooms and chicken strips.
Toast sliced sweet potato.
Top toasted sweet potato with lettuce and stir fry chicken and veggies.

As breakfast alternative I top with eggs or additive free bacon instead of chicken.

LAURA'S CREPES

INGREDIENTS:

- Makes 2!
- 2 eggs
- About 1/4 cup flax seed meal (good for milk supply)
- Big handful spinach
- 1 clove garlic
- 2 sprigs green onion
- Salt/seasonings to taste

METHOD:

Combine everything in a food processor. It should be thinner than a smoothie, but not watery.

Add water or other approved liquid if it's too thick, or more flax seed meal if it's thin. Pour about half into a preheated nonstick skillet or griddle and spread around with spatula or by tilting the pan. When the top looks dry enough, either flip the whole thing or fold in half. Fill with whatever approved things you like!

Here I've got salmon, cucumber, and hummus (since I'm out of avocado). *You can also make a "sweet" version by leaving out garlic and onion, swapping cauliflower for the spinach, and adding cinnamon, nutmeg, and almond milk (seed allowance). Tastes sort of like a French toast wrap.*

Abbie Kemp

One year on, a whole year maintaining and continuing to learn, grow and feel fitter, happier and healthier. I love this way of life now! It is a lifestyle choice. I choose to be gluten-free, dairy-free & refined sugar-free. I make the best choices when I'm out and about for meals. I only have a wine on the very odd occasion and often not even then. I love having my sparkling water as a treat for tea, & my peppermint tea and two pieces of 90% dark chocolate most nights. I now make my own peanut butter, almond butter and Sharny's chocolate sauce. So good! I call this a journey, because I continue to learn and try new things out. I love cooking with whole food ingredients for all meals, both savoury and sweet.

I love running and keeping fit! This month I am participating in my first half marathon! I know I can do it at a good pace as I have run this distance on my own.

By no means am I perfect and I still have goals for my future fit and happy self. Life still throws challenges along the way, but knowing that this lifestyle certainly helps me feel much more capable of feeling clear headed and ready to do my best everyday. Love our FitFam! Love to Sharny and Julius and the whole SJ Crew. I am also so grateful for the many wonderful friendships I have developed with people from all over the world along the way.

INGREDIENTS:
- Chicken
- Garlic
- Ginger
- Lime juice
- Rind
- Chilli
- Coconut aminos

METHOD:
Marinate chicken in garlic, ginger, lime juice and rind, chilli and coconut aminos. It was so yummy! Serve how you choose with salad or cauliflower rice.

EMILY'S CAULIFLOWER CILANTRO LIME RICE

INGREDIENTS:

- Cauliflower rice
- Lime juice
- Seasoning: cilantro, pico
- Ground turkey, lean

METHOD:

Cauliflower rice seasoned with cilantro, pico, cauliflower, and a squeeze of lime juice fried in a skillet. A side of extra lean ground turkey with Flavor God's taco seasoning, and a handful of romaine hearts.

SHARNY Ꮇ JULIUS

SARAH-JANE'S BAKED SALMON WITH ROASTED VEGGIES

INGREDIENTS:

- Salmon
- Broccolini
- Kale

METHOD:

Baked the salmon and roast the broccolini and kale. Spice it up with cinnamon and cayenne pepper.

Favourite weekend dinner in front of the fire!

JULIA'S SPICY CUCUMBER TREATS

INGREDIENTS:
- Chicken breast
- Capsicum
- Spinach
- Chilli sauce, additive free or homemade
- Cucumber

METHOD:
Chicken breast with chilli sauce, capsicum and spinach served on cucumber!

INGREDIENTS:

- Cauliflower rice
- 100g chicken breast sliced finely
- 2 Brussel sprouts sliced
- 2 asparagus chopped fairly small
- 1 teaspoon each of minced garlic and ginger (use fresh if you have it)
- 2 teaspoons of coconut oil

METHOD:

Heat lightly 2 teaspoons of coconut oil and add the garlic and ginger. Stir fry for a few seconds before adding chicken, stir fry a few seconds and then add veggies. Stir fry for about 1-2 mins and serve!

You can add a pinch of my additive free orange, garlic and chilli salt for that extra flavor!

RECIPE IDEA:
Make a hamburger with Portobello mushrooms instead of a bread bun. Add baked zucchini strips on the side. You can also make bell pepper sauce instead of ketchup!

KELLY'S CAULIFLOWER, VEGETABLE AND SALMON PUFFS

INGREDIENTS FOR STOCK:

- Cauliflower
- Salmon
- Spring onion
- Red and yellow capsicum
- 1 egg
- Nutritional yeast

METHOD:

Pre-heat oven to 180 degrees.
Cook and mash cauliflower.
Fry flaked salmon, finely chopped spring onion, red and yellow capsicum.
Add egg and nutritional yeast.
Mix well scoop up and roll into balls.

Its quite a wet mix, squash it together and bake in the oven for about 20 minutes or until lightly browned.

INGREDIENTS:

- Zucchini
- Eggs
- Bacon, additive free
- Cucumber
- Lettuce
- Spring onions

METHOD:

Breakfast idea! Make eggs in to a flat thin omelette with herbs. Grill the bacon and added cucumber, lettuce and spring onions - voila - a BLC wrap!

LEJLA'S WAFFLE SANDWICH

INGREDIENTS:

- 1 x Small eggplant
- 1 x Medium zucchini
- 4x Eggs
- Approved vegetables of choice
- Additive free spices of choice
- Filling ideas: tuna, fresh vegetables, additive free bacon

METHOD:

Blend eggplant and zucchini.
Press the liquid out them.
Place back into the blender with 4 eggs.
Fill waffle maker, cook.
Add desired fillings.

This amount is for 2-3 serves.
It works with cauliflower or capsicum too.

Sarah Ferguson

Thank you SO much for creating this program! I've tried so many nutrition and exercise programs over the years and I have lost the same 10-20 pounds so many times. It was a constant struggle, but this program is so different!

This is the fittest I've ever been in my adult life and I haven't weighed this little since high school (and I'm 43 years old)! I bought the program, on a whim, late on a Friday night and I started on the vegan program the next morning! I reached my first goal of 130 pounds by week 6, reached my dream goal of 125 by week 10 and my buffer goal of 123 by week 12! I decided to continue on (with some extra healthy carbs added in, after I hit my goal).

This is a lifestyle change for me and I am looking forward to joining the maintenance group and continuing my journey!

Starting weight: 138-140 pounds (didn't weigh myself the day I started, but had been stuck in this range for months)
Day 4 weight: 142 pounds (almost quit then, but so glad I didn't!)
Final weight: 123 pounds (I went from a size 6-8 US to a size 2 US)

RECIPE IDEA:
Combine approved veggies with coconut aminos and sesame seeds.

Easy , enjoy!

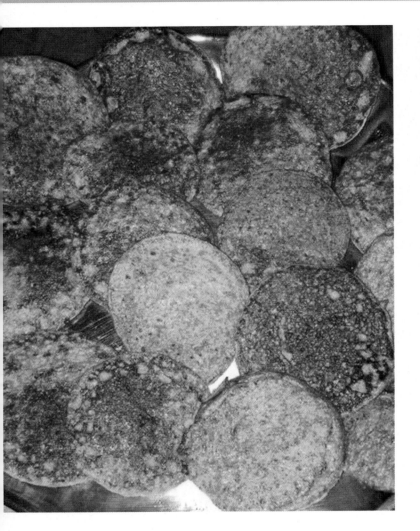

INGREDIENTS:
- Soaked (8hrs) mung beans
- Split black beans (urad dal)
- Blended with spinach garlic cumin and salt

HOW TO:
Fry pancakes in pan. Enjoy!

VEGAN PESTO INGREDIENTS:

- 1 cup fresh basil
- 20 activated almonds
- 2 cloves of garlic
- 1 tsp coconut oil
- 1 tbsp lemon juice
- 2 tbsp nutritional yeast
- Dash of salt
- 1-2 tbsp water (to thin)

METHOD:

Blend all until smooth. Serve with zoodles and Nutritional yeast. Pictured with a side of asparagus. Serves 2-4 .

"Don't focus on 8 weeks just focus on today! Remember, you're stronger than you think!"

Sandy Vecchio

I completed the program last October 2016 and have been on maintenance since. I was blessed to have found Sharny and Julius program. I was turning 50 and at the heaviest I've been in my life at 168. I had been very fit up until I was 25, then I just put the weight on. We drank wine every night with no regard and we both were so sick of how we felt.

I felt depressed and trapped. I knew how it was to be fit, but just could not get my ass back into the gym. I needed something that I could do at home and that didn't take hours at the gym.

I committed myself to the 8 weeks to do every workout - to finish. I changed the way I ate and followed Sharny and Julius eating plan to the tee!

I have maintained my weight and my current bodyfat is 19.2%. My next focus will be to add muscle and get to 14%. For all you ladies out there giving this a try half heartedly, commit yourself to finish. Don't focus on 8 weeks just focus on today! Remember, you're stronger than you think!

SANDY'S VEGGIE "CRACK"

INGREDIENTS:

- 1 red, yellow, and orange Peppers diced
- 1 onion diced
- 1 tomato diced
- 1 lime juiced and zest
- 1 large handful of Cilantro chopped
- 2 garlic garlic cloves chopped
- 1-2 jalapeño diced (remove seeds)
- 1 large cucumber diced
- White vinegar not sure how much, I use enough to bind it together.
- Salt and pepper to taste

METHOD:

Combine all ingredients and get addicted!

Vegan approved!

INGREDIENTS:
- Coriander
- Cumin
- Oregano
- Garlic powder
- Cinnamon
- Chilli powder
- Nourish approved veggies of choice.

METHOD:
Stir fry in a hot pan and enjoy!

Veggie and protein smoothie!

INGREDIENTS:

- 1 scoop Nourish approved vanilla protein powder
- 1 cup Nourish approved almond milk (soak 10 almonds overnight, drain, peel off skins, blend with 1 cup water)
- 3 cups spinach or kale
- Ice
- Add a dash of cinnamon or 1 tsp 100% cacao powder to change up the flavor!

METHOD:

Place all ingredients in mixer and whizz!

INGREDIENTS:

- 125mL unsweetened almond milk
- 2 tablespoons chia seeds
- 1 tablespoon vanilla vegan approved protein powder
- 1/4 teaspoon ground cinnamon
- 1/8 teaspoon ground ginger
- 1/4 raw carrot (coarsely grated)
- Pure vanilla bean powder (to taste)
- A pinch Himalayan salt

METHOD:

Mix into a food processor until mixed well. Pop it into a bowl/jar/container & let it sit in the fridge overnight. Serve for breakfast in the morning with a tablespoon of activated pumpkin seeds (from your morning snack allowance) for a walnut crunch substitute!

INGREDIENTS:

- 1 cup baby spinach
- 1/4 a cucumber (1/2 a Lebanese cuc)
- 1/4 cup fresh mint leaves
- 1/4 cup fresh basil leaves
- 1/2 lime, freshly juiced
- 1 cup ice
- 1 cup water
- 1/2 serve approved vanilla protein powder*
- Pinch Himalayan salt
- Pinch cayenne pepper (you can be more generous! good thermogenisis boost)

Tips:

- If you're vegan or not on nourish, add 1/4 avocado.
- You could also very easily add some celery to this, if you like.
- please note if you have this as a snack rather than breakfast, either eliminate the protein powder & add pure vanilla bean powder instead or have protein powder instead of almonds/seeds for morning snack.

CHRISTINA'S SPICY INDIAN VEGETABLES

INGREDIENTS:
- 1 tomato, diced
- 1/2 cup shallots, diced
- 1 zucchini, diced
- 1 eggplant, diced
- 1/2 capsicum, diced
- 1 packet or bunch organic fresh coriander, chopped
- 2 cups spinach leaves
- 1 tsp organic ground cumin
- 1 tsk organic turmeric
- 1 tsp organic mustard seeds
- 1/2 tsp organic chilli flakes
- 1 1/2 cups of water

METHOD:
Place all of the dry herbs into a preheated fry pan and dry cook them for approximately 2 minutes to activate and release the flavours. Stir consistently and pop the mustard seeds as your stirring. It will smoke a little, don't panic.

Stir through 1 1/2 cups of water until it is all mixed well. Add all of the diced vegetables, except the spinach leaves. Stir through diced vegetables and cook on a moderate heat and stirring regularly for approximately 20 minutes. Add spinach lives and stir. Cook and stir for 10 more minutes.

CHRISTINA'S VEGAN FRIENDLY CAJUN VEGETABLES

INGREDIENTS:

- 2 zucchinies, diced
- 2 celery sticks, diced
- 1/2 spring onoins, diced
- 2 cups red lentils
- 3 tsp organic cajun blend
- 7 cups water

METHOD:

Place all ingredients into a medium saucepan and stir until combined. Bring to the boil and then reduce heat to a simmer. Stir regularly for approximately 20-30 minutes until lentils are soft.

SWATI'S VEGAN CABBAGE TACOS

INGREDIENTS (TACOS):
- Cabbage Leaves (lightly roasted)
- Black eyed beans (boiled and seasoned)
- Tomatoes
- Cucumber
- Red onion
- Coriander
- Lemon
- Salt
- Cumin(organic additive free)

METHOD:
Lightly roast cabbage leaves.
Boil black eyed beans with tomato, cucumber, red onion, coriander, lemon, salt and cumin (to taste).
Drain.
Assemble stuffing on a base of cabbage & home made red chilli paste.

INGREDIENTS (RED CHILLI PASTE):
- Red Chilli
- Garlic
- Salt
- Cumin
- Water (as required)

METHOD:
Grind all ingredients to make into a paste. Enjoy

SHARNY ⧓ JULIUS

EMMA'S LENTIL PATTIE

INGREDIENTS:

- Cooked lentils (used 1 cup which made 6)
- Chopped coriander root
- Fine grated - 1 zucchini, 1 carrot and garlic clove
- Ground chia seed w/ water (to make chia egg
- 2 heaped tbs of ground chia with about 100ml of water)
- Hot curry powder
- Chopped baby spinach and coriander leaves
- Some seeds (sesame)

METHOD:

Mix chia and water in a bowl until it thickens, and leave until needed.

Add coriander root.

Squeeze excess juice out of carrot and zucchini and add to pan with the garlic.

Cook for a few minutes to soften.

Add the curry powder, spinach and coriander leaves and cook another min till spinach is wilted.

Remove from pan and add to cooked lentils.

Pulse the mix in a food processor till it lentils start to break down and mix gets sticky.

Add the chia egg or an egg to bind.

Hopefully, the mix is wet but not too wet that it falls apart (if that the case, add a little almond meal to absorb some of that liquid. I didn't squeeze out the zucchini juice so mine needed that.)

Roll into palm sized patties and cool or set in the fridge. You can cook them in oven or pan fry when you want to eat!

ROWAN'S HOMEMADE GF QUICHE AND BARRA

KETO

INGREDIENTS:
- Barramundi
- Eggs
- Approved veggies of choice
- Barramundi
- Broccoli
- Cauliflower
- Salt & pepper

METHOD:
Mix eggs and veggies together bake .
Throw the barra, broccoli, and cauli in the oven
(season with salt and pepper).
Serve!

JULIUS' STEAK AND MIXED VEG TOPPED WITH SIMPLE SALSA

KETO

INGREDIENTS:
- Steak of choice (grass fed beef)
- Asparagus
- Mushrooms chopped
- Tomato diced
- Leek chopped
- Zucchini sliced
- Garlic finely chopped
- Garlic chives finely chopped
- Coconut oil

METHOD:
Fry off asparagus, mushrooms leek, zucchini, garlic in a small amount of coconut oil.

Grill steak to your liking.

Place cooked vegetables on a plate, top with steak and garnish with tomato and garlic chives.

Eat.

Like most dudes, I love cooking and I especially love eating, but I hate cleaning up afterward!!! So, I turn to the BBQ for as much of my cooking needs as possible...

INGREDIENTS FOR STOCK:

- Broccoli
- Avocado
- Toasted nuts and seeds
- Green salad
- Chicken breast

METHOD:

Cooked all on the barbie... Close the hood, dishes are done! And room to cook enough for tomorrow and a steak for dinner later!

Serve with salad.

INGREDIENTS FOR STOCK:

- Cauliflower
- 100 % coconut wrap
- Cooked chicken
- Avocado

METHOD:

Is there a method? Assemble and demolish!

INGREDIENTS FOR STOCK:
- Chicken breast (you can use prawns or fish)
- Capsicum
- Mushrooms
- Zucchini
- Organic additive free Mexican spice (you could use another spice of choice)

METHOD:
Cut chicken and vegetables in even sized chunks .

Coat chicken in spice.

Skewer the chicken and vegetables alternatively.

Grill on a non stick hot grill.

Enjoy!

Simon Jago

I joined the program and went in to lose 28kgs.

Because of the great program and support, I since completed my first full marathon and am about to run a 100k ultra marathon. I have also stopped taking my depression medications and feel that is now also basically gone.

YOUR RECIPE HERE

Not only is the FitFam community waiting excitedly for you to join them, we're also all looking out for new and exciting recipes that fit within the guidelines of our programs.

If you're a bit of a kitchen aficionado, share your recipes in the group and email them to us so we could put them in the next book!

*Please make sure that....

- ☑ The recipe is yours and not copied from someone else.
- ☑ Has a beautiful photo and not like the food has been dropped on the floor. LOL.
- ☑ Has ingredients quantities and method of how it is done.

To join our programs, head to our website here:
www.sharnyandjulius.com

Made in the USA
Monee, IL
06 November 2022